SO-APM-221

LOVE SONGS

from STAGE & SCREEN

The Life, Times, & Music™ Series

LOVE SONGS
from STAGE & SCREEN

The Life, Times, & Music™ Series

Julie Koerner

FRIEDMAN/FAIRFAX
PUBLISHERS

Dedication

This one is also for my children, Matt and Jenna.

Acknowledgments

Once again, I would like to thank Ben Boyington for his important editorial input.

A FRIEDMAN GROUP BOOK

©1994 by Michael Friedman Publishing Group, Inc.

All rights reserved. No part of this publication may be reproduced, stored in a retrieval system, or transmitted, in any form or by any means, electronic, mechanical, photocopying, recording, or otherwise, without prior written permission from the publisher.

ISBN 1-56799-131-9

THE LIFE, TIMES, & MUSIC™ SERIES
LOVE SONGS FROM STAGE & SCREEN
was prepared and produced by
Michael Friedman Publishing Group, Inc.
15 West 26th Street
New York, New York 10010

Editor: Benjamin Boyington
Art Director: Jeff Batzli
Designer: Andrea Karman
Photography Editor: Jennifer Crowe McMichael

Grateful acknowledgment is given to authors, publishers, and photographers for permission to reprint material. Every effort has been made to determine copyright owners of photographs and illustrations. In the case of any omissions, the publishers will be pleased to make suitable acknowledgments in future editions.

Printed in the United States of America

For bulk purchases and special sales, please contact:
Friedman/Fairfax Publishers
Attention: Sales Department
15 West 26th Street
New York, New York 10010

(212) 685-6610   FAX (212) 685-1307

Contents

Introduction

Since the beginning of time, men and women alike have been profoundly affected by a universal emotion: love. The human brain enables us to obtain food and shelter to ensure our survival, but the heart controls the emotional strings that cause us to feel, pursue, express, celebrate, or mourn the state of being in love. All the arts, from literature to painting and sculpture, from music to drama and dance, are at their most powerful when they are communicating feelings about love.

Arising from vaudeville and burlesque, musical theatre on Broadway began as storyless singing and dancing revues.

As musical theatre evolved, story and character development became more important, but the singing and dancing—the pure spectacle of it all—has never been forgotten. This scene from *Oklahoma!*, one of the best loved musicals of all time, features an exciting ensemble dance number.

One favorite form of art and expression is song, which invites us to share the emotions evoked by music. Whether through solemn prayer, rhythmic chanting, joyous choral singing, or whistling while we work, almost all people use music to express themselves. A song can even make us feel good physically: we can shut out the world and enjoy the emotions; we can breathe more deeply and sing more loudly. Who cares how we sound? In the car, in the shower, in our dreams, we can be Tony Bennett or Ella Fitzgerald.

Early Theatre

America's first noteworthy staged musical drama—*The Beggar's Opera*, written by John Gay in 1728—came from England in 1750. A sophisticated ballad opera about social and political snobbery in England, *The Beggar's Opera* both entertained audiences and stirred up controversy with its satirical point of view. The success of *The Beggar's Opera* led to a succession of comic operas with themes borrowed from England and from France and Germany, until Americans began to create their own original musicals, known as minstrel shows.

In minstrel shows, white entertainers put on dark makeup ("blackface") to look black and imitated stereotypical black mannerisms, creating racially biased caricatures of African-Americans. (At this time, slavery still existed in

The Beggar's Opera, a musical imported from England in 1750, was the first of a series of musical dramas with themes (and in some cases, entire stories) borrowed from European playwrights and composers and re-created in North American venues.

Stephen Foster (1826–1864)

Born on July 4, 1826, in Lawrenceville, Pennsylvania, songwriter Stephen Collins Foster may have owed some of his patriotism to his date of birth. Foster was always interested in music despite his father's disapproval, and he published his first song at age eighteen. His father insisted that his son work as a bookkeeper, but Stephen spent his spare time writing songs that were performed frequently in minstrel shows, often under an assumed name. In fact, his song "Old Folks at Home" was published under the name of Edwin Christy, founder of the Christy Minstrels, who had paid Foster fifteen dollars for the tune. In his lifetime, Foster wrote as many as 189 songs, but often sold them directly to the music publisher for a flat fee; for all his prolific musical skills, Foster seemed to lack business savvy. Although Foster's life was characterized by major mood swings, his songwriting legacy exemplifies the American heritage of the nineteenth century: "Oh, Susanna!" "De Camptown Races," "My Old Kentucky Home," "There's a Good Time Comin'," "Jeanie with the Light Brown Hair," and "Beautiful Dreamer."

the United States.) Today, this period of blackface entertainment is regarded as an embarrassment, but we can try to look at it as a testimonial to the unity that can be brought to people through music and dance.

By the 1890s, the public had lost interest in minstrel shows. Audiences had begun to crave more sophisticated forms of entertainment. This led to the development of vaudeville, an eclectic performing art that was among the most popular entertainments in North America.

Both the word *vaudeville* and the form itself had their origins in France, in a small town in the vaux de Vire (the valley of Vire) that was noted for its composers of satirical songs. American vaudeville, however, had little in common with French theatre. Most often, credit for American vaudeville is given to Tony Pastor (1837–1908), who opened a theater for family entertainment in Paterson, New Jersey, in 1865. Pastor was a minstrel performer who observed the shift in audience attitudes and decided to produce entertainment that would attract women and children (audiences at this time consisted mainly of men). He prohibited the sale of alcohol, banned smoking in his theatres, and instructed all performers to keep their acts "clean" of offensive language and behavior. A vaudeville show contained a wide variety of acts, usually eight to ten but sometimes as many as twenty. Audiences might see a magician, an animal act, singers, dancers, comedians, jugglers, fire-eaters, and sports champions, all in one show. While the acts may have appeared to be in random order, the more successful producers carefully structured the order of the acts to build up the audience reaction. Many legendary performers, including Lillian Russell, Sarah Bernhardt,

Tony Pastor, a minstrel show performer turned producer, is commonly considered the father of American vaudeville.

W.C. Fields began his career as an ensemble performer on the vaudeville circuit.

W.C. Fields, George M. Cohan, Harry Houdini, Al Jolson, George Burns, Jack Benny, and Sophie Tucker, began as vaudeville performers and went on to successful theatrical careers.

For a vaudeville performer, life was grueling: shows were repeated several times a day in one city, then the company moved on to another city, where shows were also booked one after another. The songs were as varied as the performers, ranging from Mae West's "If You Don't Want My Peaches You'd Better Stop Shaking My Tree" to traditional ethnic songs like "My Wild Irish Rose" to new songs about American city life, such as "The Sidewalks of New York," written by Charles Lawler in 1894.

The success and popularity of vaudeville lasted fifty years and led to the opening of nearly four thousand theatres across North America, which employed about twenty-five thousand artists. By the early 1920s, however, radio, nightclubs, and motion pictures had begun to steal away audiences and performers, and the approaching Depression led to a decline in the interest in vaudevillian entertainment. As times became tough and audience interest waned, vaudeville gradually gave way to burlesque.

Originally, burlesque was intended as a form of satire and characteristically included both comedy and the presence of voluptuous women. Eventually, this style of bawdy music and comedy evolved into entertainment for men only, and often ended with a "Special Added Attraction," which might be anything from an athletic exhibition to a performance by an "exotic" dancer. When burlesque began to favor the bawdy over the comedic, its draw became more specific, and audiences gradually grew smaller.

Looking to attract a wider audience, entertainment producers began to create spectacular shows combining music, dance, sets, and costumes. To showcase such extravaganzas, the Hippodrome Theatre, with a stage large

A group of "Ziegfeld girls" crowd into a cramped makeup room between stage numbers during the 1936 Ziegfeld Follies.

The Hippodrome was one of the first theatres in North America to combine a fanciful stage show with the newest craze: talking pictures.

enough to accommodate six hundred performers, opened in New York. Around 1905, audiences watched fires and floods, elephants and horses, dancers and warriors perform at the Hippodrome. This was true spectacle!

By the 1920s, American theatre had adopted another French entertainment form: the revue. The revue was similar to staged burlesque in that it presented music and dance, but instead of being made up of many disjointed acts following one another, each revue was built around a central theme. One important producer of lavish revues was Florenz Ziegfeld, whose Ziegfeld Follies became more lavish and elaborate with each new production. Ziegfeld's dedication to glamour mesmerized audiences and critics alike—some of whom came to his shows just to verify whether he could outdo his previous productions!

Florenz Ziegfeld, center, in hat and mink, surrounded by members of his Follies cast.

Florenz Ziegfeld (1869–1932)

Born into a theatrical family (his father was founder of the Chicago Musical College and cofounder of the Chicago Symphony Orchestra), Florenz Ziegfeld married actress-singer Anna Held in 1897, and his first ventures as producer—*A Parlor Match* and *Papa's Wife*—were vehicles to promote his wife. In fact, Ziegfeld's first Follies, presented in New York in 1907, featured the Anna Held Girls, billed as "fifty of the most beautiful women ever presented on a single stage."

While Ziegfeld continued to work on other musical revues, he faithfully produced the Ziegfeld Follies into the 1930s, with each new version a more glamorous, more spectacular show than the one preceding it. The Follies served as a showcase, in a cosmopolitan French venue, for beautiful dancers, as well as for the talents of composers, lyricists, actors, and comics of the day.

In 1908, Follies star Norah Hayes and her husband, Jack Norworth, wrote "Shine On, Harvest Moon" for the show. Irving Berlin's name first appeared on the credits of the Follies of 1910. By 1917, the cast included Eddie Cantor, W.C. Fields, Will Rogers, Bert Williams, Dorothy Dickson, and Fanny Brice. For the 1919 Follies, Irving Berlin wrote the whole score, including the song "A Pretty Girl Is Like a Melody." In 1922, Ziegfeld added the subtitle "A National Institution Glorifying the American Girl." But by 1926, increasing expenses and impending economic disaster meant that Ziegfeld could not produce a new Follies. He tried again in 1927 with a coproducer, but the Follies were unable to generate enough excitement to sustain a new show each year.

Florenz Ziegfeld died in 1932, and while many attempts were made to re-create the Follies after his death, none were nearly as successful as those of the impresario himself. His life was dramatized in a 1936 movie called *The Great Ziegfeld*, starring William Powell and Louise Rainer; the film won the Academy Award for Best Picture, and Rainer won for Best Actress. Another film, *Ziegfeld Girl*, starring James Stewart and Judy Garland, was produced in 1941, and in 1944, prolific and imaginative MGM producer Arthur Freed made *Ziegfeld Follies*, in which Florenz looks down from heaven to produce one last masterpiece.

Ziegfeld hired many composers, including Irving Berlin, Jerome Kern, and Victor Herbert, to write songs for the Follies. Berlin's 1919 song "A Pretty Girl Is Like a Melody" became the theme song for the Ziegfeld Follies.

The 1920s also saw the development of a smaller, more intimate revue with a less elaborate production but a more imaginative or sophisticated story. In 1925, The Theater Guild Junior Players performed *The Garrick Gaieties*, featuring the first musical score written by Richard Rodgers with lyrics by Lorenz Hart, on Broadway. With the onset of the Depression, the expense and extravagance of the lavish revues became impractical, then impossible, but the smaller, more intimate revue retained its integrity and established a place for itself on the American stage.

Composer George Gershwin (seated at piano), producer Sigmund Romberg (behind Gershwin), and Florenz Ziegfeld (right) with members of the cast of *Rosalie*.

During the late 1800s, the English playwriting team of W.S. Gilbert (left) and Arthur Sullivan created many clever operettas, most of which were extremely successful in both Europe and North America.

During the same period that American producers were borrowing entertainment concepts from France, England was actively creating a successful theatrical style of its own. British poet and librettist William Schwenk Gilbert (1836–1911) and his partner, composer Arthur Seymour Sullivan (1842–1900), are most often credited with fostering modern musical theatre. Their first theatrical success was the 1875 production of *Trial by Jury*, followed in 1877 by *The Sorcerer* and in 1878 by their "overnight sensation," *H.M.S. Pinafore*. This show was first produced at the Boston Museum, then played throughout the United States with more than ninety touring companies. For many of these productions, the operetta was adapted so loosely that it was barely recognizable as originally conceived by Gilbert and Sullivan.

Musical Theatre

While all theatrical events require a producer, a director, and "stars," the success of a musical theatre production is determined by the carefully managed collaboration of still more specialized components.

A musical theatre production begins with a story and a script (called the "book"), written by the librettist, around which the music is written. The book is the skeleton of the production; it holds together the story, the dialogue, the music, and the dance, and outlines how they will work together to tell a story. A book can be written from an original idea or it can be an adaptation of an existing story. In the latter case, it is the librettist who adapts the story into the skeleton for the musical, as Oscar Hammerstein II converted the Lynn Riggs play *Green Grow the Lilacs* into the book for *Oklahoma!* and Alan Jay Lerner

A tender moment from an early production of Richard Rodgers and Oscar Hammerstein's *Oklahoma!*

As Ed Sullivan looks on, Alan Jay Lerner (second from the left) and Frederick Loewe are presented with an award commemmorating one million sales of the original cast recording of *My Fair Lady*.

wrote *My Fair Lady* from George Bernard Shaw's *Pygmalion*. The composer and the lyricist then write the play's music and the words to the songs. Sometimes one person does both jobs, as Cole Porter did in his masterpiece *Kiss Me Kate*. Sometimes two people form a partnership, like Rodgers and Hammerstein or Lerner and Loewe, that creates a collaborative magic. Quite often, the music is the most memorable component of a production. Many times, the music and songs develop a life of their own, and become successful outside the musical. Did you know that the song "More Than You Know" was written by Vincent Youmans for the short-lived musical *Great Day*?

The Composers

In any theatrical production, each member of the creative team is integral to the success of the piece. In musical theatre, the music determines the overall tone and mood of the show. The composer is responsible for creating music that elicits certain reactions from the audience. To be successful, this music must work in tandem with the story, the action, and the script. Without its great composers, musical theatre would not have the history it does, nor would it have experienced the greatness and popularity it has shown over the years.

Irving Berlin (1888 –1989)

Born Israel Baline, Irving Berlin left Russia as a young boy with his parents and eight siblings to live in New York City's "melting pot," the Lower East Side. His father died when he was nine, and Baline quit school to take odd

The unforgettable Irving Berlin smiling for the camera in a 1928 photograph.

jobs and earn money for his family. Like his cantor father, he had a pleasant singing voice, and was soon singing and making up his own words to entertain customers at the Bowery beer hall where he waited tables. In 1911, Irving Berlin, as he called himself, published lyrics to a relatively nondescript piece of music entitled "Alexander and His Clarinet." With Irving Berlin's words, this tune, now called "Alexander's Ragtime Band," became one of America's most popular songs. Berlin then began writing musical revues, beginning in 1911 with *Jardin de Paris*, which was followed shortly thereafter by *Watch Your Step*. In 1929, Berlin wrote the score for the Marx Brothers film *The Cocoanuts*. In addition to his song "A Pretty Girl Is Like a Melody," which he wrote for the Ziegfeld Follies, Berlin gave us such favorites as "Oh, How I Hate to Get Up in the Morning," "What'll I Do?" "Blue Skies," "Puttin' on the Ritz," and many, many more.

A publicity still from the Marx Brothers movie *The Cocoanuts*, for which Irving Berlin wrote the score.

Victor Herbert (1859–1924)

Victor Herbert, an Irishman who grew up in Germany, later became known as one of America's greatest composers. Classically trained, Herbert began his musical training at the piano, but later became a proficient cellist. In 1889, he composed *The Fortune Teller*, the success of which ensured his reputation as a brilliant composer. He later composed the music for *Babes in Toyland*, *Naughty Marietta*, and *Eileen*, among other operettas. In the 1920s, Victor Herbert was instrumental in the formation of the American Society of Composers, Authors and Publishers (ASCAP), which guaranteed artists and publishers recompense for their music, which had until then been used freely by anyone, at any time, for any purpose.

Jerome Kern (1885–1945)

In 1904, nineteen-year-old composer Jerome Kern approached music publisher Max Dreyfus (1874–1964) hoping to sell some of his music. Dreyfus was impressed by Kern's songs and hired the composer to work for his company, T.B. Harms. Kern's first two songs were

In addition to writing some or all of the music for more than thirty Broadway shows, composer Jerome Kern also enjoyed success in London and Hollywood.

featured in a Broadway show called *An English Diary*. Shortly thereafter, Kern went to London to work with producer Charles Frohman (1860–1915), beginning a profitable relationship with Frohman and the British theatre. His success in America increased as well: between 1905 and 1912, Kern contributed to thirty Broadway musicals. At the Princess Theatre in New York, he composed music for *Nobody Home* and *Very Good, Eddie* in 1915, *Oh, Boy!* in 1917, and *Oh Lady! Lady!* in 1918. He enjoyed a comfortable level of success on both continents until 1927, when *Show Boat* appeared on Broadway to a phenomenal reception. From then on, Jerome Kern was considered a

A farcical dance number from *Very Good, Eddie,* one of Jerome Kern's first big Broadway successes.

master by his audiences and his peers, and he wrote the music for several other

shows, including *Music in the Air, Sweet Adeline,* and *Roberta.* The 1939 play

Very Warm for May was Kern's last musical, and although it was not successful

with audiences, Kern's song "All the Things You Are" was later featured in two

Jo Stafford (1920–)

Jo Stafford had such vocal versatility that she was able to sing any style of music she chose. Her love of music and her flair for fun resulted in a broad and varied singing career. Jo became so popular during World War II that she earned the nickname "G.I. Jo." As a girl, she studied classical music, then sang with the Pied Pipers and Tommy Dorsey's orchestra. From the late thirties through the late fifties, she sang with Frank Sinatra and Gordon MacRae, and with the bands of Sy Oliver, Johnny Mercer, and Paul Weston (whom she later married). She recorded pop, folk, and novelty songs. Stafford never strove to achieve fame; in fact, she used pseudonyms for some of her recordings: as "Cinderella Stump" she parodied country mu-

sic, and as "Darlene Edwards" (with Weston as "Jonathan Edwards") she recorded several albums. Jo retired from singing in the 1960s ("Darlene," however, continued recording into the 1980s!).

Show Boat

The phenomenal success of the musical *Show Boat* was due in large part to the respectful treatment of the 1926 Edna Ferber novel on which it was based. The idea to dramatize the story about people working and traveling on a riverboat along the Mississippi River belonged to Jerome Kern, who called on Oscar Hammerstein II to write the book and lyrics for the stage production. The drama is based on the lives of the boat captain, his daughter Magnolia, the gambler Gaylord, and the riverboat entertainers Julie and her husband, Steve. The story spans several years and compellingly and poignantly portrays the tumultuous lives of these characters.

The play was produced by Florenz Ziegfeld, and opened in 1927 on Broadway to overwhelmingly favorable reviews. Many of the Kern and Hammerstein songs, such as "Can't Help Lovin' Dat Man," "Why Do I Love You?" and "Make Believe," are memorable, and "Ol' Man River" is one of the most powerful songs ever written for the theatre. *Show Boat* was produced three times on film: in 1929 it was produced as one of the earliest "talkies" (this version is now lost), and it was remade in 1936 for Universal by Carl Laemmle, Jr., and again in 1951 for MGM by Arthur Freed. Both of the films that are still in existence hold up quite well dramatically today.

Gaylord and Magnolia share a quiet moment in the first film version of *Show Boat*, produced in 1929.

films: *Till the Clouds Roll By* in 1946 and *Because You're Mine* in 1952. In 1939, Kern moved to California; in 1945 he moved back to New York to write *Annie Get Your Gun*, but he was stricken with a heart attack on a street corner and died shortly after. The score for *Annie Get Your Gun* was written instead by Irving Berlin, and is considered one of his greatest works.

Annie Get Your Gun

Among its many treasures, the Rodgers and Hammerstein musical *Annie Get Your Gun* brought us the song "There's No Business Like Show Business." In this song, Annie Oakley, played by Ethel Merman, was referring to Buffalo Bill's Wild West Show, but the song has been used as an unofficial show business theme song ever since it was first heard on stage in 1946. With book by the brother-and-sister team Herbert and Dorothy Fields and songs by Irving Berlin, who was recruited at the last minute to replace Jerome Kern after his sudden death, *Annie Get Your Gun* was an immediate, undeniable success for everyone involved. Many of the songs, such as "They Say It's Wonderful," "I Got the Sun in the Morning," "Anything You Can Do (I Can Do Better)," are cited as being among Berlin's finest.

Ethel Merman was an incomparable Annie on Broadway, and Mary Martin was a success as Annie on tour. The film version was produced in 1950 by Arthur Freed for MGM, but most critics felt that the project failed to capture the spirit of the stage play. Originally, Judy Garland had been chosen to play Annie in the film. When she didn't work out—she is said to have been fired because of her bad temperament—Doris Day and others were considered as replacements, but in the end Betty Hutton was awarded the coveted role.

Ethel Merman (1909–1984)

Ethel Merman was born Ethel Zimmerman in Astoria, New York. Even though her first job was for a vacuum-parts company, she knew she wanted to be something special; she was so confident that she would succeed in this desire that she turned down her first show business offer because it was for a part in the chorus. Her confidence, as it turned out, was well placed; soon after her refusal of the chorus part, she was hired by producer Vinton Freedley and composer George Gershwin to play a role in *Girl Crazy*, in which she sang "I Got Rhythm." The rest, as they say, is history. Although she lacked formal training, she had a powerful voice and a commanding onstage presence. Among her long string of successes were *Dubarry Was a Lady*, *Panama Hattie*, *Something for the Boys*, *Annie Get Your Gun*, *Call Me Madam*, *Anything Goes*, and her personal favorite, *Gypsy*.

Johnny Mathis (1935–)

*I*t seems that even as a youth, Johnny Mathis could do anything he chose to do. The son of a vaudevillian song-and-dance man, Mathis started his singing career at the age of thirteen. In high school, he was a champion jumper and wanted to be a physical education teacher. But he soon realized that it was music that ruled his heart, and he was discovered singing with friends at the 440 Club in San Francisco by record executive George Avakian, who recognized his talent immediately. Within a year, Johnny Mathis's tender, romantic voice, first singing jazz-style music, had sold a million records. At the request of producer Mitch Miller, Mathis turned to singing ballads, and continued to sell hit after hit, sometimes having as many as four albums in the top-selling lists.

Leonard Bernstein (1918–1990)

The great Leonard Bernstein was renowned not only as a Broadway composer but as a conductor and composer of classical music in venues all over the world.

A composer, conductor, and pianist, Leonard Bernstein was one of America's most prolific and most famous musical talents. Born in Lawrence, Massachusetts, Bernstein attracted the attention of music fans all over the world in 1943 when he conducted a nationally broadcast performance of the New York Philharmonic. Bernstein was musical director of the Philharmonic from 1958 to 1969,

Leonard Bernstein (seated at piano) leading a sing-along with the creative talents responsible for _On the Town_. From left to right: book writer/lyricist Betty Comden, actress Rosalind Russell, book writer/lyricist Adolph Green, producer George Abbott, and conductor Lehman Engel.

and in 1971 he debuted his masterpiece, a work entitled _Mass_, for the opening of the John F. Kennedy Center for the Performing Arts in Washington, D.C. Although the world probably remembers him best for having composed the music for _West Side Story_ (1957), Bernstein also wrote the music for many other stage productions and films, including _Candide_ (1956), _On the Town_ (1944), and the ballet _Fancy Free_ (also 1944).

Richard Rodgers (1902–1979)

Richard Rodgers showed an interest in music and composition as a child; he claimed that Jerome Kern's _Very Good, Eddie_ convinced him at age fourteen to write music. In 1918, Rodgers formed a partnership with lyricist Lorenz Hart that lasted some twenty-five years. Together, Rodgers and Hart wrote music and lyrics for, among others, _Fly with Me, Poor Little Ritz Girl, The Garrick Gaieties, Jumbo,_ and _By Jupiter._ Lorenz Hart had erratic work habits, but he nevertheless produced brilliant love songs; "With a Song in My Heart,"

"The Most Beautiful Girl in the World," "Where or When," "My Funny Valentine," and "Bewitched, Bothered, and Bewildered" are some of Hart's best songs. Unfortunately, Hart suffered personal problems (including alcoholism) that eventually caused work interruptions and finally a dissolution of the partnership. In 1942, Richard Rodgers found a new partner in Hammerstein II, and the new team changed the future of the musical theatre. Through the 1940s and 1950s, they wrote and produced a succession of hits—*Oklahoma!*, *Carousel*, *South Pacific*, *The King and I*, *Flower Drum Song*, and *The Sound of Music*—many of which are often revived. Hammerstein, a man of superior intellect, was a self-admitted sentimentalist, and many of his songs, such as "We Kiss in a Shadow," from *The King and I*, reflect that romantic tendency. Rodgers and Hammerstein were unusual in that their music was fully integrated into their plays—it was used to help tell the story, advance the action, express emotions, and even serve as a tool for character development. Their contributions are considered by many to mark the transition in musical theatre from pure entertainment to true art.

Anna (Gertrude Lawrence) takes notes as the King of Siam (Yul Brynner) waxes eloquent in Rodgers and Hammerstein's *The King and I*.

Foreground, from left to right: Lorenz Hart, Herbert Fields, and Richard Rodgers collaborating in Hollywood in 1929.

The King and I opened on Broadway in March 1951; it got there by taking a path opposite to that of many successful plays. *Anna and the King of Siam*, a book written by Margaret Langdon and based on the autobiography of Anna Leonowens, had been made into a movie in 1946, starring Rex Harrison and Irene Dunne. Actress Gertrude Lawrence (1898–1952) bought the rights to the Langdon story and took the project to Rodgers and Hammerstein. They conducted a search for a different actor to play the King of Siam opposite Gertrude Lawrence, and Yul Brynner was selected. Brynner's distinctive looks, presence, and powerful baritone brought an eclectic chemistry to the role, which he stayed with through the run of the play. In 1956, he played the same role in the movie musical, and won an Academy Award. He renewed his success in the 1970s with a revival tour of the play.

George Gershwin (1898–1937)

Born into a nonmusical family, George Gershwin began his musical career in what would be considered an entry-level position, as a demonstration pianist and song plugger at a publishing house in Tin Pan Alley. He wrote and promoted his own songs until the flamboyant singer Sophie Tucker (1884–1966) liked one called "If You Want 'Em You Can't Get 'Em" and helped get it published. Soon after, Gershwin took a job as rehearsal pianist for a show called *Miss 1917*, with music by Victor Herbert and Jerome Kern.

Vic Damone (1928–)

Born Vito Rocco Farinola in Brooklyn, New York, Vic Damone had his first show business job as an usher at the Paramount Theatre. His singing won him top honors on the *Arthur Godfrey Talent Scout* radio show, and he had his own radio program on CBS in the 1940s, at which time he began to record for Mercury. His striking looks helped him to obtain roles in several films, beginning with *Rich, Young and Pretty* in 1951. In the sixties he was very popular in Great Britain, but at other times he had to turn to a career in real estate to make ends meet. Over the span of several decades, Damone has had many hits, including his famous "You're Breaking My Heart," "Don't Blame Me," and "Make Someone Happy." Now married to actress-singer Diahann Carroll, Damone continues to be a popular nightclub performer.

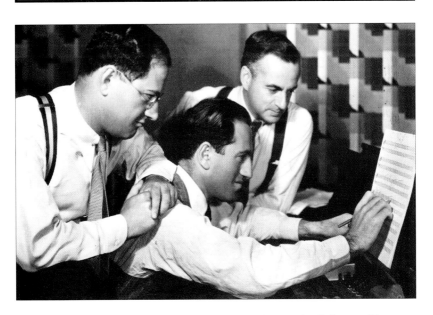

From left to right: Ira Gershwin, George Gershwin, and writer Guy Bolton working on the orchestration for the tune "Delishous" from the 1931 movie *Delicious*, starring Janet Gaynor. The music written for this film was the first Gershwin Brothers work created expressly for the screen.

Finally, he got the attention of music publisher Max Dreyfus, whose clients included Jerome Kern and Richard Rodgers. In 1919, George Gershwin was asked by producer Alex Aarons (1891–1943) to write the score for *La, La, Lucille*. This score turned out to be the most memorable feature of the play. In the meantime, Al Jolson (1886–1950) did a version of a Gershwin song entitled "Swanee," which the public liked so much that it sold more than two million records in one year. Gershwin, not one to pigeonhole himself with a particular style of music, then wrote *Rhapsody in Blue*, which was performed for the first time by the Paul Whiteman Orchestra in 1924. With his older brother Ira, who wrote the lyrics, George collaborated on *Lady, Be Good!* and several other plays, including 1927's *Funny Face*. In 1936, the Gershwins went to Hollywood to make movies. Their first film was *Shall We Dance?*, starring Fred Astaire and Ginger Rogers; the song "They Can't

Despite his lack of formal musical training, George Gershwin become one of the world's most well-known and most prolific composers.

By 1937, when *Shall We Dance?* was released, the Fred Astaire–Ginger Rogers duo had a devoted audience who typically attended every one of their films.

Take That Away from Me" was nominated for an Academy Award. The Gershwins continued to write for both stage and screen, including a film version of *Funny Face* in 1956. In addition to the song "'S Wonderful" from *Funny Face*, Gershwin wrote countless memorable love songs, including "Someone to Watch over Me," written for Gertrude Lawrence, "Embraceable You," and "But Not for Me."

Meredith Willson (1902–1984)

Another composer whose early training was in classical music was Meredith Willson, who learned to play the flute as a child in Iowa. Willson joined the Sousa Band in 1919, then played with the New York Philharmonic for five years in the 1920s.

In the early 1940s, Broadway composer Meredith Willson was musical director for NBC's *Maxwell House Coffee Time.*

Ella Fitzgerald (1918–   )

orn in Virginia, Ella Fitzgerald was orphaned when she was very young and was raised in Harlem by her aunt. As a teen, she entered a talent contest as a dancer, but got nervous at the last minute and sang a song instead. Her performance won her first prize, which was a place as vocalist in the Chick Webb Band. She stayed with the band for several years, and their first hit was "A-tisket, A-tasket." Ella traveled with Chick until his death in 1938, and then took over the band for three years. By 1942, she had begun her solo career, and she has spent the last fifty years singing and writing songs. In addition to her undisputed status as the Queen of Scat, Ella is also considered one of the greatest singers of the American song: she has recorded the songs of Harold Arlen (1905–1946), Irving Berlin, George and Ira Gershwin, Jerome Kern, and Rodgers and Hart, among many others.

Vaughn Monroe (1911–1973)

aughn Monroe grew up in Iowa singing and playing trumpet in local bands. He had aspirations to become an opera singer, but during the Depression years he continued to take jobs with professional dance bands until he formed his own in 1940. Their first hit came soon after. Monroe's deep, resonant voice, heard on the Meredith Willson song "Till There Was You," made him a very popular singer. Eventually, the band broke up and Monroe became an actor and singing cowboy.

He wrote "May the Good Lord Bless and Keep You" for the radio comedy *The Big Show*, and in 1957 had his first success on Broadway with *The Music Man*, which was made into a successful film in 1962. Many of his songs, such as "Till There Was You" and "76 Trombones," were instant hits. After several more Broadway ventures, Willson worked with Charlie Chaplin on the score of *The Great Dictator* and was nominated for an Academy Award for his score of the 1941 film *The Little Foxes*.

Vincent Youmans (1898—1946)

At age nineteen, composer Vincent Youmans caught the attention of the leader of his U.S. Navy marching band—none other than John Philip Sousa. After Youmans wrote a song that Sousa included in the band's repertoire, the young composer became determined to make a

An early photograph of Vincent Youmans, composer of such well-loved tunes as "More Than You Know" and "Tea for Two."

In *The Music Man*, Robert Preston played the lead character—a con man who tricks the residents of a small town into letting him manage a boys' band.

career of writing music. When he left the navy, Youmans approached music publisher Max Dreyfus, who hired him to write songs. Youmans' music was featured in 1921's *Two Little Girls in Blue*, then in *Wildflower*, *Mary Jane McKane*, *Lollipop*, and *No, No, Nanette*, which featured the songs "Tea for Two" and "I Want to Be Happy." Throughout the 1920s and 1930s, he continued to write musicals, most of which were later filmed, such as *Hit the Deck*, which contained the song "Hallelujah," the first piece he wrote in the navy, and 1929's *Great Day!*, featuring "More Than You Know," with words by Billy Rose and Edward Eliscu. Youmans' prolific career was cut short at age forty-seven, when he died of tuberculosis. "More Than You Know" was also featured in the films *Hit the Deck*, *Encore*, and *Funny Girl*, a biography of Fanny Brice starring Barbra Streisand.

Vincent Youmans' *Hit the Deck*, starring Ann Miller (above), Tony Martin, and Jane Powell, told the story of three sailors on leave in San Francisco.

The Hi-Lo's

*T*he Hi-Lo's were a singing group consisting of four men—Gene Puerling (1929–), Bob Strasen (1928–), Clark Burroughs (1930–), and Bob Morse (1930–)—who first sang together in December 1953 as the Encores, the vocalists with the Billy May Band. When they decided to embark on their own career, they adopted the name the Hi-Lo's because there was a great height disparity among them: Burroughs and Puerling were short; Strasen and Morse were tall. They sang together throughout the 1950s; one highlight was a tour with Judy Garland. In 1959, Strasen left the group and was replaced by Don Shelton. In the early sixties, the Hi-Lo's guested on many popular television programs, including those of Andy Williams and Rosemary Clooney, and in 1964 they sang in the Jack Lemmon comedy *Good Neighbor Sam*. The Hi-Lo's split up in 1964, each to pursue a different career.

Billy Rose (1899–1966)

*B*orn William Samuel Rosenberg, Billy Rose was an ambitious and flamboyant author, lyricist, and producer. Rose had had many jobs in the entertainment world before he collaborated on the musical scores of *Great Day!* and *Sweet and Low.* He cofounded the Songwriters' Protective Association with Edgar Leslie (1885–1976) and George W. Meyer (1884–1959) in 1931. Rose married Fanny Brice in 1929, and their seven-year marriage was the subject of several movies and books. As an entrepreneur, Rose opened Billy Rose's Music Hall in New York in 1934 and the Diamond Horseshoe in 1938. He is credited with writing the lyrics to many popular songs, including "Me and My Shadow," "Without a Song," and "It's Only a Paper Moon."

Cole Porter (1891–1964)

There is no way to discuss American musical theatre without discussing the contributions made by Cole Porter, who wrote both music and lyrics for a great number of unforgettable songs. Unlike most of his peers, Porter was born in the United States to a wealthy family. From the time of his birth in Peru, Indiana, through his years at prep schools and at Yale University, Porter showed an interest in music and song that continued at Harvard with the production of *See America First*, which even played a short run on Broadway. Porter spent the war years in the French foreign legion, and while en route to America at the end of the war he met a producer named Raymond Hitchcock (1865–1929). By the end of the journey, Hitchcock had become enamored of Porter's musical talents, and the result was the inclusion of several Cole Porter songs in Hitchcock's 1919 Broadway revue, *Hitchy-Koo.* During this time, Porter met music publisher Max Dreyfus, who was always quick to recognize new talent, and Dreyfus took Porter on as a client. Porter's first big success on Broadway was in 1928 in a show called *Paris*, featuring the song "Let's Do It," which caused Cole Porter's fame as a lyricist and composer to skyrocket. The next year

Cole Porter puts on a command performance for one of his favorite fans.

in Europe, another Cole Porter show, *Wake Up and Dream*, introduced the

song "What Is This Thing Called Love?" Cole Porter favorites include

"You Do Something to Me," "Night and Day," "I Get a Kick Out of You,"

"My Heart Belongs to Daddy," "From This Moment On," "I Love Paris,"

"In the Still of the Night," "You'd Be So Nice to Come Home To," and

"Do I Love You?"

Frank Loesser (1910–)

Born into a musical family, Frank Loesser played piano at an early age—no doubt inspired by his piano-playing father and brother—and took equal pleasure in being creative with words. In one of his early jobs, as a reporter for a newspaper in New Rochelle, New York, Loesser wrote gossip notes in clever rhyming couplets. Trying his hand in Hollywood, Loesser had a hit in the Dorothy Lamour movie *The Hurricane*: the song "The Moon of Manakoora," with music by Alfred Newman (1901–1970). In the following years, several Loesser songs, most notably "See What the Boys in the Back Room Will Have" and "Jingle Jangle Jingle," were featured in films. In 1949, Loesser wrote both music and lyrics for his first Broadway show, *Where's Charley?*, based on the novel *Charley's Aunt*, by Brandon Thomas. A farce about a man who attends a

An ensemble performance of "A Bushel and a Peck" from the 1953 production of Frank Loesser's *Guys and Dolls.*

party dressed as a woman and the lawyer who thinks "she" is socially promi-

nent and attempts to court "her," *Where's Charley?*, starring Ray Bolger, was a

big hit, and included two Frank Loesser songs: "Once in Love with Amy" and

"My Darling, My Darling." In 1950, *Guys and Dolls* reached the stage, replete

with Frank Loesser songs, including "Luck Be a Lady," "A Bushel and a Peck,"

and "I've Never Been in Love Before." Next came *The Most Happy Fella*, then

a show called *How to Succeed in Business Without Really Trying*, for which

Loesser won the Pulitzer Prize in drama, the Antoinette Perry (Tony) Award,

and the Drama Critic Circle Award, confirming him as one of musical the-

atre's most versatile creative talents.

Frederick Loewe (1904–1988)

Frederick Loewe was born in Vienna. Because his father was an operetta tenor,

Viennese operettas and waltzes were a significant part of his upbringing. He be-

gan to play the piano and compose as a child, and when he was fifteen his song

Composer Frederick Loewe (seated at piano) with his second, and most successful, partner, lyricist Alan Jay Lerner.

Left to right: director Vincente Minelli, actor Maurice Chevalier, producer Arthur Freed, lyricist Alan Jay Lerner, and actor Louis Jourdan behind the scenes at the filming of *Gigi*.

"Katrina" became popular in Europe. Loewe came to America in 1924 to pursue a concert career, but instead found himself performing odd jobs on both coasts—including boxing, delivering mail by horseback, cowpunching, and prospecting for gold. When he returned to New York to pursue his musical career, Loewe wrote for many off-Broadway ventures until he and his partner Earl Crooker got the attention of Broadway producer Dwight Deere Wiman (1895–1951). Crooker and Loewe wrote songs for Wiman's 1937 musical *Great Lady*, which had a very short run on Broadway. Loewe grew discouraged, until he hooked up with Alan Jay Lerner to rewrite some old Loewe and Crooker songs for a new play, *Life of the Party*. The play wasn't successful but the partnership was, though the fruits of their collaboration met with only moderate success until the opening of *Brigadoon* in 1947.

Set in the magical Scottish village of Brigadoon, which awakens from sleep once every hundred years, *Brigadoon* was unlike any other musical. Two Americans, Tommy and Jeff, happen to be in Brigadoon when

it awakens. Tommy falls in love and wants to stay in Brigadoon forever.
In this play, real life and fantasy are interwoven in a lyrical, surreal man-
ner. Thanks to the enchanting story and the beauty of the music and the
songs, such as "Come to Me, Bend to Me," which manage to be topical
yet reminiscent of old Scottish folk songs, *Brigadoon* was a great success.
Al Jolson made "Come to Me, Bend to Me" famous by singing it on his

radio program. The film version of *Brigadoon* was produced in 1954 by Arthur Freed for MGM, and, although it was faithful to the stage play, many critics said it lacked the original luster of the live performance. Together, the Lerner and Loewe team went on to write the music and lyrics for such productions as *Paint Your Wagon* and their greatest collaborative achievement, *My Fair Lady*.

The American visitors Tommy and Jeff (played by Gene Kelly, left, and Van Johnson) show their Scottish friends in the enchanted town of Brigadoon how well outsiders can dance.

Andy Williams (1928–)

A native of Iowa, Andy Williams, along with his three brothers, formed the Williams Brothers Quartet. The group went on to a successful radio career, joined by Kay Thompson, who sang with the quartet until 1953. Once Williams embarked on his solo career, his casual, smooth style resulted in his success in radio and later on his own television program.

My Fair Lady

Colonel Pickering (left) and Professor Henry Higgins (right) size up Eliza Doolittle's potential to be a "lady."

The theatrical version of *My Fair Lady* was the culmination of several previous versions of George Bernard Shaw's *Pygmalion*. The play was filmed under the original title by producer Gabriel Pascal (1894–1954), who had the idea to turn it into a musical, but did not have the rights to the Shaw comedy. After Shaw's death, Pascal spoke to Lerner and Loewe about making the musical and they, along with other Broadway composers and lyricists of the day, decided it was not a feasible undertaking. Several years later, after Pascal's death, Lerner and Loewe looked at the property again, and decided the time might be right to make the musical. They approached the project with the intention of departing from some of the standard conventions of popular stage musicals; they planned to write music and lyrics that would serve to advance the action of the story. The unequivocal choice to play the lead character, diction fanatic Professor Henry Higgins, was Rex Harrison, whose speaking voice was perfect, but whose singing ability was limited. *My Fair Lady* was produced on stage with virtual perfection, lasted six years on Broadway before going on tour, and continues to be revived today.

The Lyricists

While story and music can often be great alone, they reach their true height and effectiveness only when linked by the creative talent who puts words to the music, in the process creating a transition between music and script—the lyricist. The lyrics serve not only to set a mood (like the music itself) but to convey a message; later in the history of musical theatre, they also came to be used to advance the story and serve as a tool for character development. The lyricist is as essential to the success of a show as the composer; a catchy tune does little good without equally catchy (or powerful) lyrics.

Lorenz Hart (1895–1943)

Born in New York, Lorenz Hart met Richard Rodgers for the first time around

1918, and a historic partnership was formed. Their first collaboration was a

song in the play *A Lonely Romeo*, produced by Lew Fields (1867–1941), the fa-

ther of Herbert and Dorothy. The song was "Any Old Place with You."

Rodgers' musical genius and Hart's way with words combined for a career that

would include twenty-six Broadway musicals, twenty film scores, and several

London musicals. Their first full score was in 1925 for *The Garrick Gaieties*, in

which only the score was deemed memorable. The songs in this show included

A scene from Rodgers and Hart's *The Garrick Gaieties*.

Composer Richard Rodgers and lyricist Lorenz Hart in the 1930s, their most creative period.

"Manhattan," which caught on quickly with audiences, who adored the sophistication and wit that came to be characteristic of Rodgers and Hart productions. Lorenz Hart's lyrics, especially in his love songs, could be sharp, clever, and sometimes cynical; this may be because Hart's own life was marked by emotional instability. Bothered by being unusually short, Hart claimed to be unlucky in love, and his most stinging lyrics sometimes reflected feelings of unrequited love. Rodgers and Hart made major contributions to the developing sophistication of musical theatre, with songs such as "Ten Cents a Dance" (from *Simple Simon*, 1930), "The Most Beautiful Girl in the World" (from *Jumbo*, 1935), "My Funny Valentine," "The Lady Is a Tramp," "Where or When" (all from *Babes in Arms*, 1937), and "I Didn't Know What Time It Was" (from *Too Many Girls*, 1939), and with their film scores, which included "Lover" and "Isn't It Romantic" (both from *Love Me Tonight*, 1932), and "You Are Too Beautiful" (from 1933's *I'm a Bum*, in which Hart appeared).

Oscar Hammerstein II (1895–1960)

In sharp contrast to Lorenz Hart's sometimes cynical attitudes about love, Richard Rodgers' next partner was a true believer in the power of love. Born into a theatrical family (his grandfather had built opera houses and theaters, and his father had managed many theaters), Oscar Hammerstein II studied law but couldn't resist the family tradition. In the early 1920s, Hammerstein wrote thirteen musicals with Otto Harbach (1873–1963), the most memorable of which are *Rosemarie*, *Sunny*, and *The Desert Song*. In 1926, he was

Lyricist Oscar Hammerstein II (left) and composer Richard Rodgers created many outstanding musicals together, including *Oklahoma!*, *South Pacific*, and *The Sound of Music*.

Richard Rodgers (seated at piano) and Oscar Hammerstein II with Yau Shan Tung, one of the stars of their 1960 musical, *Flower Drum Song*.

approached by Jerome Kern, who wanted to produce the Edna Ferber novel *Show Boat* for the musical stage. The resulting collaboration was a stupendous success: *Show Boat* is still considered one of Broadway's greatest triumphs. Hammerstein and Kern collaborated again on *Music in the Air* in 1932, and their last venture as partners was *Very Warm for May*.

Hammerstein first collaborated with Richard Rodgers in 1943 on a musical that was originally called *Green Grow the Lilacs*. Because Lorenz Hart, whose personal life had begun to deteriorate, did not want to work on it, Rodgers turned to Hammerstein, whom he already knew and respected, and together they turned *Green Grow the Lilacs* into the Pulitzer Prize–winning *Oklahoma!* Their success seemed to increase with each new work, as they turned out one hit after another: *Carousel, Allegro, South Pacific, The King and I, Flower Drum Song,* and *The Sound of Music*. Hammerstein also won two Academy Awards, one for "The Last Time I Saw Paris," from the film *Lady Be Good*, and the other for "It Might As Well Be Spring," from the movie *State Fair*. The collaboration between Richard Rodgers and Oscar Hammerstein II was bound by mutual trust and respect; they had a policy that if Hammerstein didn't like a line of music, or Rodgers didn't approve one line of verse, those lines would be scrapped without further ado.

Ira Gershwin (1896–1983)

During the height of the Ziegfeld Follies' popularity, there was another theatrical revue company called George White's Scandals. Music publisher Max Dreyfus introduced George Gershwin to George White (1890–1968), and Gershwin wrote his first songs for Scandals. One song, "I'll Build a Stairway to Paradise," is the first noteworthy song with lyrics by George's brother Ira, who had previously written lyrics under the name Arthur Frances, a combination of two other Gershwin siblings' names. *Lady Be Good*, a movie musical starring brother-sister act Fred and Adele Astaire, was the Gershwin brothers' first musical success. They went on to write *Tip-Toes* (1925) and *Oh! Kay*, (1926), and in 1930 collaborated with George M. Cohan (1878–1942) on *Strike Up the Band*, followed in 1931 by *Of Thee I Sing*. During their thirteen-year partnership, the Gershwin brothers wrote for both stage and screen, creating some love songs that may last forever, such as "How Long Has This Been Going On?" and "They Can't Take That Away from Me."

The 1945 version of *State Fair* was a successful musical remake of a nonmusical version produced in 1933, which starred Will Rogers and Janet Gaynor.

The Goldwyn Follies

Everyone has the cure for Vera Zorina's blues in *The Goldwyn Follies*.

*T*he Goldwyn Follies was produced in 1938 by Samuel Goldwyn for his own studios, perhaps in an attempt to succeed in reproducing on film the kind of success that Florenz Ziegfeld created on the stage. The movie's plot was about a Hollywood producer's search for the "right girl" to read his scripts for him; the most interesting part of the film was its satirical point of view. The lead roles were played by Kenny Baker and Vera Zorina, and the film featured some of the top performers of the day, such as the Ritz Brothers, Edgar Bergen and Charlie McCarthy, and Buddy Clark. The *Goldwyn Follies* song "(Our) Love Is Here to Stay," written by George and Ira Gershwin, was featured again in the 1951 Academy Award—winning film *An American in Paris*, which starred Gene Kelly and Leslie Caron. *The Goldwyn Follies* was George Gershwin's last project; he fell ill while it was in production, and died shortly thereafter of a brain tumor.

Doris Day (1922–)

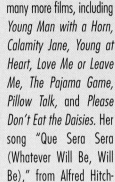

Born Doris Kappelhoff in Cincinnati, Ohio, Doris Day was the quintessential "girl next door"—she had the wholesome looks, sound, and poise that marked her as the all-American ideal. She originally wanted to be a dancer, but she turned to singing after breaking her leg at age fourteen. Her career began on Cincinnati radio with Barney Rapp, who changed Doris' last name to Day. By 1940 she had sung with the Bob Crosby Band and then moved to the Les Brown Orchestra, with whom she recorded "Sentimental Journey," the song that became her theme. Her first movie role was in *Romance on the High Seas* (1948), in which she sang songs written by Sammy Cahn and Jule Styne. This role launched her movie career, and she went on to star in many more films, including *Young Man with a Horn, Calamity Jane, Young at Heart, Love Me or Leave Me, The Pajama Game, Pillow Talk,* and *Please Don't Eat the Daisies.* Her song "Que Sera Sera (Whatever Will Be, Will Be)," from Alfred Hitchcock's *The Man Who Knew Too Much,* won the 1934 Academy Award for Best Song. Her song "(Our) Love Is Here to Stay," by George and Ira Gershwin, is from the 1938 movie *The Goldwyn Follies.*

Alan Jay Lerner (1918–1986)

Alan Jay Lerner was a writer for radio when Frederick Loewe approached him to collaborate on a remake of a play called *The Patsy*. The result of their first collaboration was retitled *Life of the Party* and was followed quickly by two more unremarkable plays, *What's Up?* and *The Day Before Spring*. The music and lyrics for their pet project, *Brigadoon*, left audiences stunned by the beauty, folksiness, lyricism, and sophistication that could be found in a story that successfully combined a Scottish fantasy with New York City reality. On the heels of their *Brigadoon* success, Lerner and Loewe wrote *Paint Your Wagon*, a musical set in America's Old West. A story about a mining camp during the Gold Rush of the 1800s, *Paint Your Wagon* was a stage hit that featured, among many beautiful songs, "They Call the Wind Maria." When Lerner and Loewe wrote the songs for one of Broadway's greatest musicals, *My Fair Lady*, they etched their names on Broadway forever. *My Fair Lady* was followed in 1957 by the film *Gigi*, and the partners returned to Broadway in 1960 with *Camelot*, a musical adaptation of the T.H. White novel *The Once and Future King*. *Camelot*, which did not experience the critical success of *My Fair Lady*, was the last collaboration of Lerner and Loewe. Alan Lerner went on to team with Burton Lane to write *On a Clear Day You Can See Forever*, and with Andre Previn to write the music and lyrics for *Coco*.

Betty Comden (1915–) and Adolph Green (1915–)

By the 1940s, the musical comedy was a popular vehicle for the Broadway stage. A new writing team, Betty Comden and Adolph Green, reworked the Leonard Bernstein/Jerome Robbins ballet *Fancy Free*, which opened on Broadway as *On the Town* and featured Robbins' balletic choreography. Next,

At the risk of breaking a few piano keys, Adolph Green and Betty Comden display the inimitable sense of humor that informed each of their shows.

Tony Bennett

Born Tony Benedetto in Queens, New York, Tony Bennett had a smooth, silky voice that enabled him to pursue a career as a nightclub singer and recording artist for Columbia. Many of his hit songs, including "Because of You," "Rags to Riches," and especially "I Left My Heart in San Francisco," are so distinctive that listeners can only imagine one voice, that of Tony Bennett, singing them.

also with Robbins, the Comden-Green team wrote *Billion Dollar Baby*, a parody of the 1920s. In 1953 Comden and Green worked with composer Leonard Bernstein and writers Joseph Fields (1895–1966) and Jerome Chodorov (1911–) on the lyrics to the musical *Wonderful Town*, based on a play called *My Sister Eileen*. The writing team then collaborated with Jule Styne to write *Two on the Aisle*, *Peter Pan*, and *Say, Darling*; in 1956, they had their biggest hit, *Bells Are Ringing*, which starred Judy Holliday, who was also in the popular 1960 movie of the same name. Two of the Comden-Green songs, "Just in Time" and "The Party's Over," became hits that are still recorded by various artists today. The Broadway version of *Peter Pan*, starring Mary Martin as Peter, was not the great success we remember until it was filmed for television, which made it so popular that it was then reproduced on stage. In the 1960s, Comden and Green teamed again with Styne, this time to write the score for *Hallelujah, Baby!* and *You're a Good Man, Charlie Brown*.

Dorothy Fields (1904–1974)

As an actress-turned-lyricist, Dorothy Fields contributed to both stage and screen. The lyricist of the popular songs "The Way You Look Tonight" and "Lovely to Look At," Fields also wrote the lyrics for *Up in Central Park*,

Jimmy McHugh and Dorothy Fields in the studio.

which turned out to be the last production of producer Sigmund Romberg (1887–1951). With her brother Herbert (1897–1958), Dorothy wrote the lyrics to Irving Berlin's songs in *Annie Get Your Gun*. In the mid-1960s she collaborated with Cy Coleman to write the lyrics for one of Bob Fosse's hit shows, *Sweet Charity*, starring Gwen Verdon and featuring the hits "Big Spender" and "If My Friends Could See Me Now." She also wrote lyrics for movies and collaborated with Jerome Kern on five films. Fields also enjoyed a lengthy partnership with Jimmy McHugh; they began by writing revues that were performed at the Cotton Club. For *Blackbirds* in 1928, they wrote the song that became their first hit, "I Can't Give You Anything But Love," and went on to pen "On the Sunny Side of the Street" and "I'm in the Mood for Love," from the film *Every Night at Eight*, produced in 1935 by Walter Wanger and directed by Raoul Walsh .

Rosemary Clooney (1928–)

Rosemary Clooney began singing in high school, and by 1949 she was a popular vocalist, recording for Columbia and performing on the television show *Songs for Sale*. By 1951, she had recorded a song that made her a star and remained a hit for decades, "Come On-a My House." Clooney appeared in four films in the 1950s, including the seasonal favorite *White Christmas* in 1954. She continued to record through the sixties, and still makes occasional appearances.

Jimmy McHugh (1894–1969)

Jimmy McHugh began his career as a pianist with a classical background, then became a composer. Besides his work with Dorothy Fields, McHugh composed the score for many Hollywood films through the 1930s and 1940s, including *Singing the Blues*, *Flyin' High*, *The Prizefighter and the Lady*, *Dinner at Eight* (for which he and Fields wrote "Don't Blame Me"), *Roberta*, *Banjo on My Knee*, *Road to Reno*, *Moon over Las Vegas*, *Jam Session*, and *Doll Face*. In the 1950s, McHugh founded a music publishing company.

Sammy Cahn reclines on a piano and reviews a composition as Saul Chapin looks on.

Sammy Cahn (1913–1993)

One of Broadway's most prolific and productive lyricists was Sammy Cahn. Born in New York City, Sammy learned to play the violin at an early age. By the 1930s, Cahn was leading a dance band with Saul Chapin; their theme song, "Rhythm Is Our Business," was recorded by Jimmie Lunceford, who had one of the top dance bands of the day. One of Cahn's first hits was "Until the Real Thing Comes Along," recorded by Andy Kirk. For the film business in Hollywood, Sammy Cahn collaborated with Jule Styne to write "I'll Walk Alone," "It's Magic," "The Tender Trap" (from the movie of the same name), and "Three Coins in the Fountain" (the theme from the movie of the same name), which won the Academy Award for Best Song in 1954. Cahn and Styne also wrote the score for the Broadway show *High Button Shoes*. With Jimmy Van Heusen, Cahn wrote several songs for Frank Sinatra, including "Love and Marriage," "Saturday Night Is the Loneliest Night of the Week," "My Kind of Town," "September of My Years," and "All the Way," the last from the movie *The Joker Is Wild*, which also starred Sinatra.

Jule Styne (1905–)

At eight years old, Julius Stein (who later changed the spelling to Jule Styne) moved with his family from London, England, where he was born, to Chicago. By the time he had reached his teens, Styne had a career as a successful pianist and was leading his own band at the Bismarck Hotel in Chicago. He worked successfully at writing and arranging music and even as a vocal coach in Hollywood. Jule Styne collaborated with many lyricists, including Frank Loesser, Sammy Cahn, and Stephen Sondheim (1930–). Some of his most memorable compositions are "Just in Time," "Papa, Won't You Dance with Me," "Diamonds Are a Girl's Best Friend," "Small World," "Make Someone Happy," "People," and "Time after Time." Jule Styne wrote the scores for many stage productions (some of which were later filmed), including *High-Button Shoes*, *Gentlemen Prefer Blondes*, *Bells Are Ringing*, *Gypsy*, and *Funny Girl*. Among his numerous credits for film scores are *Angels with Broken Wings*, *Sleepy Time Gal*, *Follow the Boys*, *Anchors Aweigh*, *Stork Club*, *It Happened in Brooklyn*, *The West Point Story*, *My Sister Eileen*, and *Three Coins in the Fountain*. Jule Styne's most recent project was writting the music for the Broadway show *Red Shoes*.

Frank Sinatra (left) rehearses a tune for the movie musical *It Happened in Brooklyn* with the assistance of director Richard Whorf (second from left), composer Jule Styne (seated at piano), and lyricist Sammy Cahn.

Lena Horne (1917–)

*L*ena Horne's throaty voice and stunning looks have made her one of America's favorite vocalists. Born in Brooklyn, New York, Horne began her career as a dancer at the Cotton Club, then sang as a solo vocalist with the Charlie Barnet Band for a year. Horne has also performed in several movies, including *Panama Hattie*, *Stormy Weather*, *Thousands Cheer*, *Till the Clouds Roll By*, *Meet Me in Las Vegas*, *Death of a Gunfighter*, and *The Wiz*. She has performed on stage and on television, toured

Europe and North America many times, and still appears whenever and wherever she chooses.

Lena Horne and Bill Robinson in the 1943 movie *Stormy Weather*, which was based on Robinson's career.

Jimmy Van Heusen (1913–)

Born in Syracuse, New York, James Van Heusen was an accomplished pianist and singer by the time he was a teenager, but his father encouraged him to go to college and become a businessman. In college, Jimmy wrote many shows with Harold Arlen's brother Jerry, and through this connection, Jimmy found himself in Chicago writing a Cotton Club revue. Eventually, he collaborated with Jimmy Dorsey on "It's the Dreamer in Me," and thereafter, most of his songs were hits. Van Heusen wrote the scores for many films, including *Going My Way*, a film that won many Academy Awards in 1944, including one for Best Song, Jimmy's "Swingin' on a Star" (with lyrics by Johnny Burke). Some of Van Heusen's many other movie scores include *A Connecticut Yankee in King Arthur's Court*, *Young at Heart*, *Anything Goes*, *Indiscreet*, *Hole in the Head*, *Say One for Me*, *Pocketful of Miracles*, *Papa's Delicate Condition*, and *Thoroughly Modern Millie*.

From the Stage to the Screen

By the late 1920s, Hollywood producers were beginning to discover that there was much money to be made from talking pictures. In 1929, the movie *Hollywood Revue* was advertised as "All talking! All singing! All dancing!" *Hollywood Revue* showcased many of the MGM studio's talents, including Norma Shearer, Jack Benny, Buster Keaton, Laurel and Hardy, and Joan Crawford.

Audrey Hepburn dances in style in the 1956 Hollywood musical *Funny Face*.

The success and commercial popularity of musical theatre led to a series of Hollywood remakes, beginning in 1950 when MGM producer Arthur Freed made a successful film version of *Annie Get Your Gun* (for which Adolf Deutsch and Roger Edens received the Academy Award for Musical Direction). In 1954, a film version of *Brigadoon* was produced, again by Arthur Freed at MGM. The 1950s also saw the film productions of *Funny Face* and *The King and I*, the latter winning Academy Awards for its star, Yul Brynner (who also starred in the Broadway version) and for Alfred Newman and Ken Darby, the musical directors. In Paramount's 1957 version of *The Joker Is Wild*, "All the Way," by Jimmy Van

Heusen and Sammy Cahn, won the Academy Award for Best Song. Arthur Freed produced *Bells Are Ringing* in 1960, and in 1962 Meredith Willson's *The Music Man* was produced by Warner; musical director Ray Heindorf won the Academy Award. Lerner and Loewe's My *Fair Lady* was produced in 1964 and received many accolades: Academy Awards were given to the movie for Best Picture, to George Cukor for Best Director, and to Harry Stradling for photography.

Above: New York's Astor Theatre was one of the most popular venues for movies such as the "All talking! All singing! All dancing!" musical *Hollywood Revue.*

Above: Although the movie musical reached its peak during the 1950s, the 1970s saw a resurgence of movies of this kind, among them *Funny Girl,* starring Barbra Streisand.

Suggested Listening

Irving Berlin

Cheek to Cheek (*Top Hat*, 1935)

How Deep is the Ocean?; Let's Face the Music and Dance (*Follow the Fleet*, 1936)

I've Got My Love to Keep Me Warm (*On the Avenue*, 1937)

Be Careful, It's My Heart (*Holiday Inn*, 1942)

They Say It's Wonderful (*Annie Get Your Gun*, 1946; with Dorothy Fields)

Cole Porter

You Do Something to Me (*Fifty Million Frenchmen*, 1929)

What Is This Thing Called Love? (*Wake Up and Dream*, 1929)

Night and Day (*The Gay Divorcee*, 1932)

I Get a Kick Out of You (*Anything Goes*, 1934)

In the Still of the Night (*Rosalie*, 1937)

Vincent Youmans

Tea for Two (*No, No, Nanette!*, 1925)

Through the Years (*Through the Years*, 1932)

Orchids in the Moonlight (*Flying Down to Rio*, 1933)

Without a Song (*Great Day!*, 1929; with Billy Rose and Edward Eliscu)

Rodgers and Hart

Isn't It Romantic? (*Love Me Tonight*, 1932)

My Romance (*Jumbo*, 1935)

My Funny Valentine; Where or When (*Babes in Arms*, 1937)

This Can't Be Love (*The Boys from Syracuse*, 1938)

I Didn't Know What Time It Was (*Too Many Girls*, 1939)

Jule Styne

Small World (*Gypsy*, 1959; with Arthur Laurents and Stephen Sondheim)

Just in Time (*Bells Are Ringing*, 1956; with Betty Comden and Adolph Green)

The Charm of You (*Anchors Aweigh*, 1945; with Sammy Cahn)

Time After Time (*It Happened in Brooklyn*, 1947; with Sammy Cahn)

Jimmy McHugh and Dorothy Fields

On the Sunny Side of the Street (*International Revue*, 1930)
I Can't Give You Anything But Love (*Blackbirds*, 1928)
I'm in the Mood for Love (*Every Night at Eight*, 1935)
Lovely to Look At (*Roberta*, 1935; with Jerome Kern)

Jimmy Van Heusen and Sammy Cahn

Love and Marriage (*Our Town*, 1955)
High Hopes (*Hole in the Head*, 1959)

Sammy Cahn

Until the Real Thing Comes Along, 1936
Saturday Night is the Loneliest Night of the Week, 1944

Rodgers and Hammerstein

People Will Say We're in Love (*Oklahoma!*, 1943)
If I Loved You (*Carousel*, 1945)
Hello, Young Lovers (*The King and I*, 1951)

All at Once You Love Her (*Pipe Dream*, 1955)
I'm Gonna Wash That Man Right Outa My Hair (*South Pacific*, 1949)

Jerome Kern

You Are Love (*Show Boat*, 1927)
I've Told Ev'ry Little Star; The Song Is You (*Music in the Air*, 1932)
The Touch of Your Hand (*Roberta*, 1933)
The Way You Look Tonight (*Swing Time*, 1936; with Dorothy Fields)

George and Ira Gershwin

Someone to Watch Over Me (*Oh, Kay*, 1926)
Embraceable You; But Not for Me (*Girl Crazy*, 1930)

Lerner and Loewe

On the Street Where You Live; I've Grown Accustomed to Her Face (*My Fair Lady*, 1956)
If Ever I Would Leave You (*Camelot*, 1960)

Bibliography

Ewen, David. *George Gershwin: His Journey to Greatness*. Westport, Conn.: Greenwood Press, 1977.

Gammond, Peter. *The Oxford Companion to Popular Music*. New York: Oxford, 1991.

Gill, Brendan. *Cole: A Biographical Essay*. Robert Kimball, ed. New York: Delta, 1994.

Kislan, Richard. *The Musical: A Look at the American Musical Theater*. Englewood Cliffs, N.J.: Prentice Hall, 1980.

Lerner, Alan Jay. *The Musical Theater: A Celebration*. New York: McGraw-Hill, 1986.

Suskin, Steven. *Opening Night on Broadway*. New York: Schirmer Books, 1990.

Taylor, Deems. *Some Enchanted Evenings: The Story of Rodgers and Hammerstein*. New York: Harper, 1953.

Suggested Reading

Bordman, Gerald. *American Musical Theater: A Chronicle*. Oxford, 1992.

Ewen, David. *Composers for the American Musical Theater*. New York: Cornwall Press, 1968.

Jackson, Arthur. *The Best Musicals: From Show Boat to A Chorus Line*. New York: Crown, 1977.

Mander, Raymond, and Joe Michenson. *Musical Comedy: A Story in Pictures*. New York: Taplinger Publishing, 1970.

Index

Photography Credits

Archive Photos: pp. 2, 15, 28–29, 31
  top, 44, 46–47, 48, 56, 57, 66
Archive Photos/Hackett: p. 31
  bottom
Archive Photos/London Daily
  Express: p. 54
Frank Driggs: pp. 9, 10, 14, 19, 20,
  27, 29 top, 34, 35, 37 top, 38,
  39, 45, 58, 60, 62, 63
FPG International: pp. 6, 12, 25

Lester Glassner Collection/Neal
  Peters: pp. 11, 21, 22 top, 23, 32,
  41, 49, 50–51, 52, 67 top
The Kobal Collection: p. 64
Northwind: pp. 8, 16
Neal Peters Collection: pp. 18, 26
  bottom, 53, 67 bottom
Photofest: pp. 7, 13, 17, 22 bottom,
  26 top, 33 bottom, 36–37, 42–
  43, 59, 61, 65
Photofest/Jagarts: pp. 24, 30, 33 top,
  55